Nita Mehta's
ALL TIME FAVOURITE SNACKS

This book belongs to SONIA SALUJA

NITA MEHTA
B.Sc. (Home Science), M.Sc. (Food & Nutrition)
Gold medalist

3A/3 Asaf Ali Road New Delhi -2

NITA MEHTA'S ALL TIME FAVOURITE SNACKS

© Copyright 1995 Nita Mehta

All rights reserved with the author.
No portion of this book shall be reproduced, stored in a retrieval system, or transmitted by any means, electronic, mechanical, photocopying, recording or otherwise, without the written permission of the publishers. While every precaution has been taken in the preparation of this, the publisher and the author assume no responsibility for errors or omissions. Neither is any liability assumed for damages resulting from the use of the information contained herein.

First Edition 1995

ISBN 81-86004-04-1

Colour Photography by **Amitava Dass Gupta**

Layout and laser typesetting :

Distributed by :
THE VARIETY BOOK DEPOT
A.V.G. Bhavan, M 3 Con Circus
New Delhi 110 001

Published by :

3A/3 Asaf Ali Road New Delhi -2

Printed at :
Nu tech Photolithographers.

Other books by the same author

Nita Mehta's VEGETARIAN WONDERS
Nita Mehta's PANEER ALL THE WAY
Nita Mehta's PERFECT VEGETARIAN COOKERY
Nita Mehta's DESSERTS & PUDDINGS
Nita Mehta's VEGETARIAN CHINESE CUISINE
Nita Mehta's DAL & ROTI

Published by
SNAB Publishers
3A/3, Asaf Ali Road, New Delhi 110 002
Telephone: 3277782, 3252948; Fax: 3277782

With Love
to
My dear daughter
Bhavna
who has always been my
official taster and critic.

No Problem!

What shall I give him to eat this evening? Something light & refreshing! The answer to your everyday problem is right here. The male - whether he be a husband or a son, finds satisfaction, both of the mind and stomach, when offered well prepared snacks after a hectic day. Rightly said, "The way to a man's heart is through his stomach." So head for these simple, light and creative snacks and prepare seven different snacks on all days of the week.

I have arranged the snacks in such a manner, that it becomes easy for you to choose the right one. The unfried snacks are low in calories and can be offered daily without the dinner being disturbed. The Indian snacks are a little heavy and thus may be relished at high tea parties. Cocktail snacks are included to serve as appetizers before a formal dinner.

Last but not the least, I would like to express my gratitude to my dear husband, Subhash, who has constantly encouraged me and made me closer to my students and several other readers through my books.

Nita Mehta

Contents

UNFRIED SNACKS 11
- Spicy Bean Puff 12
- Submarine Sandwich 14
- Mini Masala Kulcha 16
- Tomato-Coriander Rounds 21
- Steamed Moong Balls 22
- Corn Cups 24
- Pinwheels 26
- Instant Dhokla 28
- Chow Mein 30
- Idli 32
- Toast Bonanza 34
- Pea Turnovers 38
- Instant Suji Utthapam 40
- Corn Toasts 42
- Dieter's Sizzler 44
- Spinach Frankie 47

INDIAN SNACKS 49

- Channa Masala with Bhatura 50
- Bhature 52
- Kasoori-Methi Pyaz Pakoras 55
- Pao-Bhaji 56
- Upma Matar Wala 58
- Dahi-Bhalle 60
- Medu Vadai 62
- Bharvaan Aloo Tikki 64
- Til ke Cheese Toasts 66
- Saboodana Tikki 67
- Gobi Samosa 68
- Poha 70
- Potato Pancakes 74
- Kalmii Kabab 76

CONTINENTAL SNACKS 77

- Stuffed Potatoes with Corn 78

Russian Sandwiches 80
Mexican Burrito 81
Cheese Corn Balls 84
Paneer Balls with Stirf Fried Vegetables 86
Bread Patties 88
Stuffed Spinach Loaf 90
Grilled Mushroom Toasts 92
✓ Vegetable Cutlets 94
Spinach & Mushroom Pie 96

COCKTAIL SNACKS 99

Vegetable Shami Kababs 100
Beans Mornay 102
Cheese & Potato Rolls 103
Gingerly Paneer 104
✓ Rice & Cheese Puffs 105
Kale Channe ke Kababs 106
Chilli Paneer 108
Vegetable Roll-Ups 110

Fruit & Vegetable Platter 113
Vegetable Gold Coin 114
Cocktail Sticks 116
Paneer Rolls 118
Cheesy Fingers 120
Chilli Potatoes 121

REFRESHING CHAATS 123

Aloo Chaat 124
Corn Chaat 126
Peanut Chaat 128
Vegetable & Fruit Chaat 129
Potato Baskets 130

DIPS & CHUTNEYS 132

Yoghurt Minty Dip 133
Instant Imli si Khatti Chutney 134
Poodina Chutney 135
Coconut Chutney 136

Important Tips
which you must go through!

- Always take out fried food on paper first to remove excess oil. Brown paper or paper napkins may be used.
- Fry cutlets, tikkis or rolls to a dark brown colour if you want a crisp covering. Be careful not to burn them.
- Always keep cabbage handy. A small green leaf in between a sandwich or finely shredded cabbage sprinkled over the snacks makes them more appetising.
- Never throw away the sides of sandwiches or stale bread pieces. These can be dried, crushed & sifted to make crumbs.
- Bread crumbs may be added to almost any mixture of a snack if it is soft and difficult to handle. Bread crumbs make the balls, cutlets, rolls, etc. firmer, without making them heavy.
- To steam food, put food in a metal sieve over a pan of boiling water and cover the sieve. The pan should be smaller than the sieve.
- Boiled potatoes with their jackets; keep fresh for 3-4 days in the refrigerator. Keep them handy as they can be of great use sometimes.

Unfried Snacks
for all evenings

Spicy Bean Puff

Picture on page 18

<u>Servings 4</u>

2 burger buns
½ cup red rajmah (kidney beans) - soaked overnight
¼" piece ginger - chopped finely
1 onion - chopped finely
few sprigs green coriander - chopped finely
4 tbsp grated processed cheese
2 tbsp oil or butter
2-3 green chillies - chopped finely
1 tbsp tomato sauce
¼ tsp pepper

1. Pressure cook soaked beans in 1½ cups water with ½ tsp salt. Give one whistle and then keep on low flame for ½ hour.
2. Mash hot beans to a **rough** paste with a potato masher.
3. Cook paste with all ingredients for 2-3 minutes on low flame. Add salt to taste. Keep paste aside.

4. Cut buns into two halves horizontally and scoop each piece of bun a little, leaving ½ " rim on all sides.
5. To serve, apply some butter or oil on the bun halves. Heat on a non-stick pan or tawa. Press the buns on the hot tawa till the buns gets heated and turn soft & a little brown on the sides.
6. Spread the hot rajmah paste on the hot bun halves in the scooped portion as well as the sides. Sprinkle cheese on top. Sprinkle some red chilli powder on the cheese & dot with tomato sauce. Garnish with a coriander leaf. Serve.

Submarine Sandwich

Picture on page 36
Servings 2

2 hot dog buns (long buns)
2-3 lettuce or cabbage leaves
2 firm tomatoes
2 processed cheese slices - cut into 2 pieces
or
50 gms cottage cheese (paneer) - cut into 4-5 slices
1 boiled potato - cut into thin slices
salt & pepper to taste

1. Half the tomatoes. Cut into slices. Keep aside.
2. Tear each lettuce or cabbage leaf with the hand into two big halves.
3. Heat 2-3 tbsp on a tawa or a non stick pan. Fry potato slices till crisp and golden. Remove from oil.
4. Divide the bun into two halves with a sharp knife. Heat the bun halves on the non stick pan or tawa in 1 tbsp oil. Keep pressing the buns while they are being heated so that they become soft.

5. Meanwhile heat the cabbage leaves on the side of the bun on the tawa for a few seconds. Put the cheese slices on the hot cabbage leaves on the tawa and not directly on the tawa. Put the tomato slices also on the hot tawa. Shut off the fire.
6. Remove buns and green leaves with the cheese, fom the tawa.
7. Keep lettuce leaves with the cheese, on the lower bun, such that they show outside the bun from the sides.
8. Cover with potato slices. Sprinkle some salt & pepper.
9. Arrange hot tomato slices overlapping each other on the potatoes, along the whole length of the bun. Sprinkle salt and pepper.
10. Cover with the second piece of bun. Serve.

Mini Masala Kulcha

Servings 15

DOUGH
250 gms maida (plain flour)
¼ tsp dry yeast
¼ tsp baking pd.
150 ml (1 small cup) warm milk
1 tsp salt
1 tsp sugar
1½ tsp oil
1 tbsp curd

FILLING
1 small bunch of fresh poodina (mint) leaves
or
2 tbsp dried poodina leaves
½ tsp ajwain (thymol seeds)
½ tsp salt
½ tsp red chilli pd.

Spinach Frankie : Page 47

1 big onion - very finely chopped
2 tbsp chopped coriander leaves
150 gms (1 cup grated) paneer (cottage cheese)

1. Dissolve yeast in 2-3 tbsp of warm water in a cup. Keep aside.
2. Sift maida. Add sugar and salt.
3. Put curd in the centre of the maida and sprinkle baking powder on the curd. Mix baking powder with curd gently with a spoon. Leave for a few seconds till it starts bubbling.
4. Add oil and the dissolved yeast. Knead with enough warm milk to a dough. The dough should neither be too soft nor too stiff. It becomes loose after it is kept away for a few hours.
5. Grease a polythene, brush the dough with oil. Keep the dough in the greased polythene, cover it with a pan inverted over it, to keep it warm. Keep in the sun or a warm place for 3-4 hours.
6. The dough swells. Knead it again. Keep dough aside.
7. To prepare the filling, chop washed mint leaves. Mix all other ingredients, except paneer, of the filling together with the mint leaves.

Spicy Bean Puff : Page 12

8. Grate paneer finely on the filling. Mix it gently, taking care not to mash it.
9. Make lemon sized balls of the dough. Roll out. Put 1 tsp of filling in the centre. Cover to form a ball again.
10. Roll out to a diameter of 3" - 4" or desired size. Sprinkle filling all over.
11. Press gently with the rolling pin (belan) and then with your fingers.
12. Stick in a heated tandoor by applying water on the back side of the kulcha. Cook till brown spots appear. Serve hot with tea.

Note : If the kulcha falls off from the gas tandoor, scrub the tandoor well with a detergent and a metal scrubber. If it becomes difficult to remove the kulcha from the tandoor, grease the tandoor with oil first, and then wipe off the excess oil with a clean cloth. The first few kulchas are difficult to cook, but keep practising till you perfect the art of using the tandoor.

Tomato-Coriander Rounds

Servings 8

4 slices bread - toasted
2 small firm red tomatoes
salt - pepper to taste
50 gms paneer (cottage cheese)
2 tbsp finely chopped coriander
butter or margarine - enough to spread

1. Choose a firm type of bread. Toast the slices.
2. Cut into rounds or diamonds or hearts with a cutter or a sharp edged bottle cap.
3. Apply butter or margarine on the sides as well as the top.
4. Roll the sides of the bread in finely chopped coriander.
5. Place a tomato slice on the bread piece.
6. Grate some paneer over the tomato slice. Sprinkle some salt and pepper.
7. Keep in a hot oven for 3-4 minutes. Serve immediately.

Steamed Moong Balls

<u>Servings 20 balls</u>

BALLS
1 cup dhuli moong dal (split green beans) - soaked for 2 hours
1 tsp salt
4 tbsp oil

SAUCE
2 tbsp oil
3 onions - chopped
2 tomatoes - chopped
½" ginger piece - grated
2 green chillies - chopped
½ tsp salt
¼ tsp garam masala (mixed spices)
¼ tsp red chilli pd.

1. Soak dal for 2 hours. Grind with minimum amount of water to a smooth paste.
2. Cook dal in 4 tbsp of oil in a karahi for about 10 minutes on slow fire by sprinkling water occasionally.
3. Cook till dal is dry. Add salt.
4. Make marble sized balls with greased hands. Keep moong balls aside.
5. To prepare the sauce, heat 2 tbsp oil in a non-stick karahi.
6. Add onions. Cook till golden brown.
7. Add chopped tomatoes. Cook for 3-4 minutes.
8. Add ginger & green chillies.
9. Add salt, garam masala and red chilli powder. Add 2-3 tbsp of water. Cook for 1 minute.
10. Add the balls. Mix well.
11. Serve sprinkled with chopped coriander.

Corn Cups

<u>Servings 16 cups</u>

8 slices - fresh bread
½ tin (1 cup) sweet corn - cream style
1 onion - chopped finely
2 tbsp chopped coriander
2 green chillies - chopped finely
1 tsp lemon juice
1 tbsp butter
1 tbsp oil
salt to taste
¼ tsp pepper
chilli sauce to serve

1. Stamp out rounds from the slices of the bread with a biscuit cutter of 2" diameter. Roll these rounds a little with a rolling pin (belan).
2. Grease a muffin tray with butter.
3. Put one round piece of bread in each cavity. Press well.

4. Butter the round piece of bread.
5. Bake in a hot oven at 250°C for 20 minutes or until crisp.
6. To prepare the filling, heat oil. Add the onions and cook till they turn transparent.
7. Add the corn, chillies, coriander, lemon juice, pepper and salt. Cook for 2 minutes. Keep aside.
8. Fill the baked bread cases with a little corn mixture.
9. Bake again at the same temperature for 10 minutes.
10. Dot with chilli sauce. Serve.

Note : The bread cases and corn mixture can be prepared well in advance. Store the bread cases in an air-tight tin.
If you like, butter toasted slices sparingly, cut into 4 small triangles. Place a spoonfull of hot corn mixture on each piece. Serve immediately.

Pinwheels

Servings 20-25

4 slices bread - fresh
cheese spread or butter - enough to spread
2 small kheera (cucumbers)
¼ cup vinegar
1 tsp sugar
½ tsp salt
¼ tsp pepper

1. Scrape kheera. Cut into four pieces lengthways.
2. Mix salt and sugar in vinegar. Give it one boil. Sprinkle over kheera and leave for 5-10 minutes. Keep aside.
3. Roll each bread slice on a chakla with a belan, pressing firmly. Roll till holes disappear. Cut the sides of bread.
4. Spread either cheese spread or butter over the bread slices. Spread butter generously at the end so that the roll is fastened properly.
5. Put a long kheera piece at the end of each slice.

6. Sprinkle pepper on the kheera and bread.
7. Roll up the slice tightly, around the kheera.
8. Put the roll in a plastic bag and roll the bag tightly. Chill in the refrigerator for 1 hour.
9. Remove from bag and cut into ¼" slices. Serve cold.

Note : Only fresh bread (bought on the same day) can be rolled properly, such that the holes disappear and neat pinwheels can be prepared.

Instant Dhokla

Servings 10

250 gms (3 cups approx) besan (gram flour)
½" piece ginger
2 green chillies
1½ tsp salt
1½ tsp sugar
a pinch of hing (asafoetida)
¼ tsp haldi (turmeric powder)
½ tsp red chilli powder
1½ tsp citric acid
1½ tsp mitha soda (soda bicarb)

GARNISHING
a small piece of fresh coconut - grated
1 small bunch coriander

TEMPERING (CHHOWNK)
2 tsp oil
1 tsp sarson (mustard seeds)

2 green chillies - slit lengthways
1 tsp lemon juice
¼ cup water

1. Grind ginger & green chillies together to a paste.
2. Mix besan, salt, sugar, haldi, hing, ginger-chilli paste.
3. Add enough water to get a thick batter. Beat well, preferably with an electric egg beater.
4. Keep a small pan half filled with water to boil. Keep a rice steel sieve (chhanni) over the pan of water such that the steam can escape through the holes.
5. Mix citric acid to the ready batter. Mix well. Add soda. Mix very well.
6. Grease a thali. Fill half with the dhokla batter. Sprinkle red chilli pd. Keep thali in the sieve, placed over the boiling water. Cover the sieve.
7. Steam for 15 minutes. Insert a knife to check if it is cooked.
8. Cut into squares. Keep aside.
9. Heat 2 tsp oil. Add mustard seeds. When they splutter, add green chillies. Add lemonjuice & water. Boil. Pour oil over the dhokla.
10. Serve garnished with grated coconut & chopped coriander.

♣

Chow Mein

Servings 4

100 gms chow noodles
1 onion - shredded or cut into thin long strips
1 capsicum - shredded
1 cup shredded cabbage
1 carrot - shredded
¼ tsp ajinomoto - optional
½ tsp pepper
2 tsp soya sauce
1 tbsp vinegar
1½ tsp chilli sauce
2 tbsp oil
3/4 tsp salt

1. Boil 6 cups water with 1 tsp oil and 1 tsp salt. Add noodles. Cook uncovered for 2-3 minutes. Do not over cook.
2. Strain through cold water several times. Strain. Keep in the strainer for 15 minutes. Apply 1 tsp oil on the strained noodles. Keep aside.

3. Heat oil. Add onions. Stir fry for ½ minute.
4. Stir fry carrots and capsicum for ½ minute. Add cabbage.
5. Add salt, pepper & ajinomoto.
6. Add boiled noodles. Add vinegar & chilli sauce.
7. Add soya sauce. Stir fry for 1 minute. Add more soya sauce for a darker colour.
8. Serve hot with chopped green chillies in vinegar.

Idli

Servings 20

2 cups sela rice (parboiled rice)
½ cup permal rice (ordinary quality rice)
1 cup dhuli urad dal (split black beans)
2 tsp salt or to taste

1. Wash and soak both rice together for 6-8 hours or overnight. Clean, wash and soak dal separately.
2. Next morning, grind dal separately to a very fine batter till it turns whitish and absolutely smooth.
3. Grind rice also to a fine batter, but it is coarser than the dal batter.
4. Combine dal and rice batters to get a batter of a pouring consistency which is slightly thick. Add salt, beat well and keep it for 8-10 hours in a warm place, depending upon the season to make the batter sour. If the batter does not rise properly, keep it for a longer period.
5. When the batter rises and smells a little sour, it is ready. **Do not beat or stir the ready batter.**

6. Place a piece of thin wet cloth over the mould by passing the cloth through the centre pin of the mould. Fill with idli batter.
7. Put some water in a pressure cooker or a big pan, put the mould inside and cover it, without weight/whistle. Steam for 10 minutes on high flame and again for 10 minutes on low flame. Remove from fire.
8. Remove idlies from the cloth over the mould after 3-4 minutes. Serve hot with coconut chutney as given on page 136.

Note : To check if idlies are ready, insert a knife. If it comes out clean, idlies are done.

Do not stir the fermented batter which rises because of the air inside it, as it is the trapped air which makes the idli soft and fluffy.

The idli batter should not be thick, otherwise the idlies turn out hard.

Toast Bonanza

Servings 8

200 gms pizza cheese
1 small cabbage
3-4 firm tomatoes - cut into slices
2 big boiled potatoes
250 gms paneer (cottage cheese)
salt, pepper to taste
3-4 tbsp butter
8 bread slices

1. Cut paneer and potatoes into thin slices.
2. Heat 2 tbsp butter in a non-stick pan. Put a slice of potato on it and then shift to the side. Turn when the under side is light brown.
3. Repeat with the other potato slices.
4. Put some more butter. Saute the paneer lightly in 1 tsp butter.
5. Lightly toast the bread slices. Remove crust. Butter them.
6. On each toast spread a cabbage leaf.

Potato Pancakes : Page 74

7. Place 2 potato slices on the cabbage leaves. Sprinkle salt, pepper.
8. Place paneer slices to cover the potatoes.
9. Place tomato slices over the paneer.
10. Grate cheese over the toast to cover the tomatoes almost completely.
11. Grill in a preheated oven for about 5 minutes till the cheese melts and gets browned a little.

Note: Use only pizza cheese, i.e. the type of cheese should be such that it melts on heating.

Pea Turnovers

Servings 12

SHORT CRUST PASTRY (DOUGH)
200 gms maida (plain flour)
100 gms salted butter - cut into small cubes and chilled
pinch of salt
pinch of baking powder
7 tsp cold water
½ tsp ajwain

FILLING
1 onion - chopped finely
1½ cups shelled peas - boiled
1 green chilli - finely chopped
¼ tsp red chilli powder
¼ tsp garam masala (mixed spices)
salt to taste
1 tbsp oil

1. Sift flour, salt & baking powder. Add ajwain.
2. Rub butter gently with a fork into the flour till the flour starts resembling fine bread crumbs. Avoid using hands, because the heat of the hands will make the pastry tough on baking.
3. Sprinkle ice cold water over the maida. Knead lightly with minimum handling. Chill the dough for at least 15-20 minutes in a polythene bag.
4. Prepare the filling by cooking onions in oil till transparent.
5. Add green chillies & boiled peas.
6. Add salt, red chilli powder and garam masala.
7. Cook for 1 minute. Keep filling aside.
8. Make marble sized balls of the dough.
9. Roll each into 2½ inches diameter.
10. Place the prepared filling on one side & fold the other side over it.
11. Seal using a fork. Brush with milk.
12. Bake for 15-20 minutes at 200°C in a preheated oven.

Instant Suji Utthapam

Servings 4

BATTER

1½ cups suji (semolina)
1½ cups sour curd
3/4 cups water
¼ tsp mitha soda (soda bi-carb)
1 tsp salt
1 tsp red chilli powder
½ tsp garam masala (mixed spices)

TOPPING

2 tomatoes - finely chopped
2 onions - finely chopped
2 tbsp chopped coriander
1 green chilli - finely chopped
½ tsp salt or to taste

1. Sift suji. Add curd, salt, red chilli powder & garam masala. Beat well.
2. Add enough water to get a smooth, thick batter. Add mitha soda and beat thoroughly for 3-4 minutes.
3. Mix all ingredients of the topping and keep aside.
4. Heat a non-stick pan. Spread 1 tsp oil in the centre. Pour ¼ of the batter (2 karchhies approx.) in the pan. Spread, but see that it does not become too thin, otherwise it will break when you turn it.
5. Cook on low flame. When the upper side is slightly cooked, sprinkle some topping on it. Press. Pour 2 tsp oil on the sides and the top.
6. Turn only when the underside gets crisp and brown, otherwise the utthapam might break while turning.
7. Continue to cook on low flame till the onions turn light brown. Remove from pan and serve hot with coconut chutney as given on page 136.

Corn Toasts

Servings 20

1 cup (½ tin) sweet corn - cream style
1 tbsp butter
4 tbsp (1 cube) grated cheese
4 tbsp milk
2 green chillies - finely chopped
1 tsp pepper powder
1 tbsp coriander leaves
2 pinches of baking powder
salt to taste
4 thick slices of sandwich bread - lightly toasted

1. Heat butter, add tinned corn, cheese, milk, green chillies and salt.
2. Stir and simmer till the liquid is absorbed. Add coriander leaves and pepper. Mix well.
3. Remove from heat and add baking powder.
4. Butter the lightly toasted bread. Cut into 4 small triangles.

5. Apply the mixture over bread pieces, only on one side and bake with a dot of butter on top for 5-7 minutes.

Note : The left over tinned corn may be kept in a stainless steel box in the freezer compartment of the refrigerator for over a month, without getting spoilt.

When using fresh corn, select 2 tender fresh corns, boil in water or milk without salt till tender and grate them.

Dieter's-Sizzler

Servings 4

2 tomatoes
¼ tsp each of salt & pepper

PANEER BALLS

100 gms paneer (cottage cheese) - grated or mashed
1 tbsp chopped coriander
1 green chilli - chopped
½ tsp red chilli pd.
½ tsp amchoor (dried mango pd.)
¼ tsp salt
1 tsp til (sesame seeds)

MUSHROOM MASALA

100 gms fresh mushrooms - boiled
2 small onions - cut into fine rings
½ tsp lemon juice
2 tsp oil

¼ tsp salt
¼ tsp each of pepper & garam masala

SPROUTED MASALA
1½ cups sprouted moth
1 onion - chopped finely
1 green chilli - chopped finely
¼ tsp salt

1. To prepare paneer balls, grate paneer & mash it well. Add green chillies & coriander.
2. Make 8 balls.
3. Mix salt, amchoor & red chilli pd. together. Roll the prepared paneer balls in them. Keep aside.
4. To prepare mushroom masala, boil 3 cups water with 1 tsp salt. Add whole mushrooms. Boil, partially covered, for 5 minutes. Strain. Cool mushrooms. Chop into small pieces.
5. Heat 2 tsp oil on a tawa. Add onions. Cook till onions turn light brown.

6. Add mushrooms & other ingredients. Cook for 3-4 minutes.
7. To prepare the sprouted masala, steam sprouts with 1/3 cup water along with chopped green chilli, onion and salt in a pressure cooker. Keep the cooker on fire only till the first whistle is about to come. Remove from fire as soon as the whistle starts.
8. Cut tomatoes into two pieces. Sprinkle salt & pepper on them.
9. At serving time, heat the tawa.
10. Put ½ tsp oil; slow down the fire, then put til (sesame seeds). Roast for 1-2 minutes. Do not let them turn brown. Roll paneer balls on it so that they get coated with til.
11. Keep some hot mushroom masala, a little sprouted masala & 1 tomato piece along with the paneer balls.
12. Serve immediately.

Spinach Frankie

Picture on page 17
Servings 14

DOUGH

2 cups maida (plain flour)
1 potato - boiled and grated
½ tsp salt
2 tsp oil
milk - to knead

FILLING

4 cups chopped palak (spinach)
1 onion - chopped finely
a pinch of mitha soda (soda-bicarb)
2 green chillies - chopped
4 tbsp mashed paneer (cottage cheese)
2 tbsp oil
½ tsp each of salt, red chilli powder & garam masala

SEALING PASTE

2 tbsp maida dissolved in 3 tbsp water

3 tsp amchoor (dried mango pd.)
2 onions - finely chopped

1. Sift maida and salt together. Add finely grated potato.
2. Add 2 tsp oil. Knead with a little milk to a soft dough. Keep aside.
3. Make 14 small, marble sized, balls. Roll out into very thin chappatis.
4. Cook like a chappati, on both sides, on a tawa (griddle). Keep aside.
5. To prepare filling, heat oil. Add onions, cook till onions turn transparent.
6. Add chopped palak, green chillies & mitha soda. Cook for 5-7 minutes on low flame, till palak gets cooked. Add salt, red chilli powder, garam masala & paneer. Mix well. Remove from fire.
7. Mix amchoor in 6 tsp water. Spread this amchoor paste on each chappati. Sprinkle some chopped onion over it.
8. Spread palak mixture over it. Roll the chappati.
9. Join the edges with the sealing paste.
10. Heat 1-2 tbsp oil on a tawa & cook the rolled chappati in oil on low flame, till light brown. Serve hot.

Indian Snacks
for high tea parties

Channa Masala with Bhatura

CHANNA MASALA

1 cup channa kabuli (Bengal gram)
2 tbsp channe ki dal (split gram)
2 moti illaichi (big cardamom)
1" stick dalchini (cinnamon)
2 tsp tea leaves tied in a muslin cloth or a tea bag
¼ tsp mitha soda (soda bicarb)
1" piece ginger
1 green chilli
1½ tsp anardana (pomegranate seeds) powdered
2 onions - chopped finely
1 big tomato - chopped finely
½ tsp garam masala
1 tsp channa masala
1 tsp dhania powder
salt & red chilli powder to taste
4-5 tbsp oil

1. Soak channa & channe ki dal with moti illiachi, dalchini, tea leaves, ¼ tsp soda, and enough water, overnight or for 6-8 hours in a pressure cooker.
2. Pressure cook all the ingredients together to give one whistle. After the first whistle, keep on low flame for about 20 minutes. Keep aside.
3. Grind ginger, green chilli and anardana to a paste. Keep aside.
4. Heat oil. Add onions. Cook stirring till they turn dark brown. (Do not burn them). Add chopped tomatoes. Cook & mash occasionally till they turn brownish in colour.
5. Add dhania powder and red chilli powder. Cook for ½ minute.
6. Add ginger paste. Cook for ½ minute.
7. Remove tea bag and the whole spices from the boiled channas and add to the onion masala. Mix well. Add salt. Cook for 5-7 minutes.
8. Add garam masala and channa masala. Mix well. Keep on low flame for 10-15 minutes.
9. At serving time, heat 2 tbsp oil on a tawa. Toss 1 tomato cut into 2 halves and 1 green chilli slit lengthways; for a few seconds in it. Add ½ tsp red chilli pd. and pour over the hot channas in the serving dish.

♣

Bhature

Servings 10

250 gms (2 cups) maida (plain flour)
100 gms (1 cup) suji (semolina)
½ tsp mitha soda (soda-bicarb)
½ tsp salt
1 tsp sugar
½ cup sour curd
oil for deep frying

1. Soak suji for 15 minutes in water, which is just enough to make it wet.
2. Sift salt, soda and maida. Add sugar, soaked suji & curd. Knead with enough warm water to make a dough of rolling consistency.
3. Knead again with greased hands till the dough is smooth.
4. Brush the dough with oil. Keep the dough in a greased polythene and keep it in a warm place for 3-4 hours.
5. Make 8-10 balls. Roll each ball to an oblong shape, stretch a little and deep fry in hot oil. Do not let them turn brown.

Cocktail Sticks : Page 116

Kasoori Methi-Pyaz Pakoras

<u>Servings 12-14 pakoras</u>

1 cup besan (gram flour)
3/4 tsp red chilli pd.
¼ tsp mitha soda (soda-bicarb)
½ tsp garam masala (mixed spices)
salt to taste - 3/4 tsp approx.
2 small onions - sliced finely
4 tbsp kasoori methi (dry fenugreek leaves)
¼ tsp ajwain (thymol seeds)

1. Mix besan, red chilli pd, mitha soda, garam masala, ajwain & salt with enough water to a thick batter. Beat well till the mixture is smooth.
2. Add kasoori methi and onions. Mix well.
3. Deep fry pakoras to a light golden colour. Keep aside.
4. At the time of serving, press the fried pakoras slightly & refry in hot oil till brown and crisp.

Mexican Burrito : Page 81

Pao Bhaji

Servings 6

250 gms (3 big) boiled potatoes - mashed roughly
100 gms (1 cup) shelled peas
250 gms (1 small flower) cauliflower - chopped finely
250 gms (1 small flower) cabbage - chopped finely
250 gms (4 big) tomatoes - chopped finely
250 gms (3 big) onions - chopped finely
1" piece ginger
4-6 flakes garlic - optional
2 dry red chillies
2 tbsp Pao-Bhaji masala
50 gms butter
4-5 tbsp oil
salt to taste (1½ tsp)
1 tbsp chopped coriander

1. Chop all vegetables finely. Mash potatoes roughly.
2. Pressure cook cauliflower and cabbage with ¼ cup water for 2-3 minutes.

3. Grind ginger, garlic and chillies to a paste.
4. Heat oil. Add onions and cook till transparent.
5. Add peas and cook covered, till tender
6. Add ginger paste and cook for 2-3 minutes.
7. Add pao-bhaji masala and salt.
8. Add tomatoes and cook for 5-7 minutes. Mash them well, while they are being cooked. Sprinkle 2-3 tbsp water occasionally, when the vegetable is on fire.
9. Add pressure cooked vegetables and potatoes. Cook for a few minutes. Mash well while cooking.
10. Add butter and chopped coriander. Keep bhaji aside.
11. Slice 2 small onions finely. Sprinkle some salt, red chilli powder & lemon juice to taste.
12. To serve, cut buns (pao) into halves. Heat a tawa or a non-stick pan. Put 1 tbsp butter on it. Press the paos in butter, heating till they turn soft. Serve with hot bhaji, dotted with butter.
13. Serve onions mixed in lemon juice along with pao-bhaji.

♣

Upma Matar Wala

Servings 6

1½ cups suji (semolina)
½ cup oil
1 tsp sarson (mustard seeds)
1 tsp jeera (cumin seeds)
2-3 dried red chillies
1½ tbsp channe ki dal (split gram)
1 tbsp urad dhuli dal (split black beans)
2 onions - chopped finely
3½ cups water
½ cup shelled, boiled or frozen peas
juice of 1 large lemon
1½ tsp salt
10-12 curry leaves - optional

1. Roast suji in a karahi on low flame, stirring continuously, for about 5 minutes. Do not let it change colour.
2. In a clean heavy bottomed karahi, heat oil. Add jeera and sarson together.
3. When these splutter, switch off the fire. Add the red chillies & dals.
4. Stir till dals turn light brown. Return to fire.
5. Add onions. Fry till brown.
6. Add water. Add peas, salt & lemon juice. Boil water.
7. Cover and cook on low flame for 5-7 minutes till the dal is cooked and is no longer crunchy.
8. Add suji gradually with one hand and stirring with the other hand continuously, keeping the flame low.
9. After all the suji has been added fry the upma for 2-3 minutes.
10. Add 2 more tsp oil & fry some more. Serve hot.

Dahi Bhalle

Servings 12

BHALLAS
1 cup urad dhuli dal (split black beans)
½" piece ginger
1 green chilli
2 pinches of hing (asafoetida)

DAHI (CURD)
½ kg (2½ cups) curd
1 tsp powdered sugar
1 tsp roasted jeera (cumin seeds) powder
½ tsp red chilli powder
½ tsp kala namak (rock salt)
salt to taste

1. Clean, wash dal. Soak in water for just two hours. Do not over soak.
2. Strain. Grind with minimum amount of water along with the other ingredients of the bhallas.

3. Beat batter thoroughly with an electric egg beater or with hand. Keep adding 1 tbsp of water, a few times, while beating.
4. The mixture should look whitish & frothy and a ball of this mixture should float when dropped in water.
5. Heat oil to medium hot temperature.
6. Wet the back side of a katori (small bowl) by dipping in water.
7. Place a ball of the dal mixture on the wet katori. Push a kishmish into the ball. Flatten the ball. Gently slip the bhalla into the oil.
8. Deep fry 5-6 pieces at a time on low flame.
9. Heat 6 cups of water with 2 tsp salt. Remove from fire. Drop 4-5 fried bhallas. Leave in water for ½ minute. Turn them. Remove from water after a few seconds. Squeeze them gently. Keep in the fridge.
10. Beat curd very well, preferably with an electric egg beater.
11. Add all the other ingredients. Chill the prepared dahi.
12. Dip the prepared bhalle in dahi and arrange in a dish.
13. Pour extra dahi on top, at the time of serving. Garnish with ginger shreds & coriander. Serve with khatti chutney as given on page 134.

♣

Medu Vadai

Servings 20

2 cups urad dhuli dal (split black beans)
3 green chillies - finely chopped
½" piece ginger - finely chopped
2 big onions - chopped finely
2 tbsp chopped coriander
salt to taste
2 tbsp besan (gram flour)
oil for deep drying

1. Clean, wash and soak dal for 2 hours only. Do not over soak.
2. Strain the dal, add ginger and green chillies. Grind to a fine paste using the minimum amount of water in the mixer.
3. Add the onions, coriander, besan and salt to taste to the dal paste.
4. Beat the mixture with an electric egg beater for 2-3 minutes or with the hand for at least 4-5 minutes. (This step is important).
5. Heat oil to medium hot.

6. Wet the palm of your left hand, place a ball of the dal, wet the first finger of the right hand and make a hole in the vada.
7. Wet your right hand fingers, gently invert the vada on the right hand fingers.
8. Carefully slip the vada into the moderately hot oil with the help of the thumb. Do not fry on high flame.
9. Fry 6-7 vadas together, till golden brown.
10. Serve with coconut chutney as given on page 136.

Bharvaan Aloo Tikki

Servings 6

4 boiled potatoes - medium size
2 slices of bread
1 tsp red chilli pd.
½ tsp garam masala (mixed spices)
salt to taste
½ tsp chaat masala

FILLING

1/3 cup urad dhuli dal (split black beans)
½ tsp haldi (turmeric pd.)
1 tbsp oil
½" ginger - chopped finely
1 green chilli - chopped finely
1 tbsp chopped coriander
½ tsp garam masala & red chilli pd.
salt to taste
a pinch of hing (asafoetida)
½ tsp chaat masala

1. Boil 3 cups of water with ½ tsp salt and ½ tsp haldi. Add cleaned & washed dal. Boil on low flame for about 20 minutes, till dal gets cooked. Strain the dal. Keep boiled dal aside.
2. Mash potatoes. Remove crust of bread slices and dip in water. Immediately remove from water. Squeeze well to remove water.
3. Mix potatoes, bread, red chilli pd, garam masala, chaat masal & salt.
4. Heat 1 tbsp oil. Add hing. Add ginger, chopped coriander and green chillies. Add boiled dal. Add chaat masala, garam masala, salt and red chilli powder. Cook for 2-3 minutes on low flame.
5. Make balls of big size with the potato mixture. Flatten each ball. Make a slight depression in the centre. Put 1 tbsp of dal filling in the centre.
6. Form a ball again. Flatten to form a tikki.
7. Heat 1/3 cup oil in a non-stick pan or a tawa. The oil should not be too much.
   Fry only 2-3 pieces at one time. Shallow fry till brown and crisp.
8. Remove from oil on paper. Slit the tikki horizontally. Pour poodina chutney & instant khatti chutney on it, as given on pages 135 & 134.

Til ke Cheese Toasts

Servings 12

3 tbsp cheese spread or grated processed cheese
1½ tbsp maida (plain flour)
3/4 cups milk
a pinch of chilli powder
¼ tsp mustard powder
¼ tsp salt
2 tbsp til (sesame seeds)
3 slices bread
oil to fry

1. Heat milk till hot but not boiling. Lower heat and stir in flour.
2. Add cheese, chilli powder, mustard powder, salt and 1 tsp sesame seeds. Stir until cheese melts. Remove from fire.
3. Remove sides of bread. Cut each piece into four.
4. Heat oil. Dip bread pieces into the prepared sauce, then sprinkle some sesame seeds on top. Deep fry till light brown. Serve hot.

Saboodana Tikki

Servings 15

3 potatoes - boiled and mashed
½ cup mashed or grated paneer
3 slices bread - dipped in water and squeezed
½ cup saboodana (sago)
15 kishmish (raisins) - soaked in water
1 tbsp thick malai (milk topping)
1 tsp salt
½ tsp each of red chilli pd, garam masala & amchoor
1 tbsp chopped coriander
oil - enough to fry

1. Soak saboodana in water for 20-25 minutes till it turns soft. Drain off excess water by keeping in a strainer.
2. Mix potatoes, bread, paneer, salt, all spices and coriander.
3. Spread saboodana on a tray. Make balls of potato paneer mixture.
4. Flatten each ball. Put a drop of malai and one piece of kishmish.
5. Make into tikkis carefully. Roll each tikki in saboodana. Press.
6. Deep fry 3-4 pieces at one time. Serve hot with poodina chutney.

Gobi Samosa

Servings 8-10

DOUGH
3/4 cup maida (plain flour)
¼ tsp salt
2 semi heaped tbsp of ghee (vanaspati) or margarine

FILLING
1 medium cauliflower - grated
2 small boiled potatoes - mashed coarsely
¼" piece ginger - grated
½ tsp red chilli pd.
salt to taste
3/4 tsp roasted jeera pd. (cumin seeds)
3/4 tsp garam masala (mixed spices)
¼ tsp amchoor (dried mango pd.)
1 tbsp broken cashewnuts
1 tbsp kishmish (raisins)
2 green chillies - finely chopped
¼ tsp sugar

1. Mix all ingredients of the dough.
2. Add a few tbsp of water and knead to form a semi hard dough.
3. Keep dough covered for ½ hour.
4. To prepare the filling, heat 3 tbsp of oil. Put off the fire. Add ginger. Add salt, red chilli powder, garam masala, jeera, and amchoor.
5. Return to fire. Add nuts. Cook for a few seconds.
6. Add potatoes. Cook for ½ minute.
7. Add cauliflower. Mix well. Add sugar and green chillies.
8. Cover and cook on slow fire till the cauliflower is cooked. Make the filling spicy. Keep aside.
9. Make lemon sized balls of the dough. Roll out thinly. Cut into two.
10. Fold each half into a triangle to form a cone.
11. Seal the cone by applying water. Fill 1 tbsp of the filling in the cone.
12. Make a small fold or pleat on the side, opposite to the joint.
13. Now close the cone with water. Press the side opposite to the pointed side against a plate, giving it a samosa look.
14. Heat oil. Deep fry 8-10 pieces at a time on low heat.

Poha

Servings 2

2 cups chirwa (flaked rice)
1 potato - boiled & cut into small cubes
2 tbsp roasted peanuts or ¼ cup boiled peas
3 tbsp oil
2 pinches hing (asafoetida)
¼ tsp sarson (mustard seeds)
1 sprig of curry leaves - optional
¼ tsp haldi (turmeric powder)
½ tsp salt
¼ tsp red chilli pd
1 green chilli - chopped finely
2 tbsp chopped coriander
juice of ½ lemon

1. Put flaked rice in a strainer and wash it under running water for a few seconds till it gets soaked. Do not soak too much. Drain. Keep aside in the strainer.

Vegetable & Fruit Chaàt : Page 129

2. Heat oil. Add hing, then splutter sarson. Add curry leaves and haldi.
3. Add salt and red chilli powder.
4. Add potatoes, peas or peanuts & green chilli. Cook for a few seconds.
5. Add flaked rice. Cook with occasional stirring till dry.
6. Stir carefully so that the grains remain separate and unbroken. Add lemon juice. Mix.
7. Serve garnished with chopped coriander leaves.

Paneer Balls with Stir Fried Vegetables : Page 86

Potato Pancakes

Picture on page 35
Servings 4

PANCAKES

4 potatoes - medium size
6 tsp cornflour
1 tsp salt
¼ tsp haldi (turmeric pd.)
½ tsp dhania (coriander pd.)
¼ tsp red chilli pd.
2 green chillies - finely chopped
½ tbsp finely grated ginger

FILLING

2 small carrots - grated
½ cup shelled peas - boiled
¼ tsp jeera (cumin seeds)
3/4 tsp salt - to taste
½ tsp dhania (coriander) pd
¼ tsp red chilli pd.

¼ tsp garam masala (mixed spices)
a pinch hing (asafoetida)
2 tbsp oil

1. Peel, wash & grate potatoes. Add salt. Keep aside for 5 minutes.
2. When the potatoes leave water, squeeze out the water completely.
3. Mix all the other ingredients of the pancake. Keep aside.
4. To prepare the filling, heat 2 tbsp oil in a heavy bottomed karahi. Add jeera and hing. Add salt. Add grated carrots. Add dhania powder, garam masala and red chilli pd. Cook for 3-4 minutes on low flame. Remove from fire.
5. Heat a non-stick pan. Add ½ tbsp oil. Put ¼ of the potato pancake mixture and spread it with the back of a katori (small bowl) into a small pancake.
6. Put some oil on the sides and over the pancake.
7. Turn carefully when the under side is a little brown. Put the prepared filling on the cooked side. Press. Cook till the other side is done.
8. Take out the pancake carefully on to a plate. Serve hot.

Kalmi Kabab

Servings 15 pieces

1 cup channe ki dal (split gram) - soaked for 3 hours
2 green chillies - chopped finely
½" ginger piece - chopped finely
1 small potato - chopped finely
1 onion - chopped finely
2 tbsp finely chopped poodina (mint) leaves
3/4 tsp coarsely crushed pepper corns (saboot kali mirch)
1 tsp salt
¼ tsp red chilli pd, garam masala & amchoor

1. Strain soaked dal. Grind dal with just a few tbsp of water to a fine paste. Mix all other ingredients with the dal.
2. Add 1 tsp hot oil also to the paste. Beat well for 5 minutes.
3. Make 3 balls. Flatten them so that they are ½" thick.
4. Deep fry to a light pink colour. Cool for 15-20 minutes.
5. At serving time, Cut each kabab into 4-5 long pieces with a sharp knife. Deep fry these long pieces to a golden brown colour.

♣

Continental Snacks
An interesting change from the routine!

Stuffed Potatoes with Corn

Servings 6

6 big potatoes
1 tbsp soft butter
4 tbsp (1 cube) grated cheese
½ tsp salt
½ tsp pepper

FILLING
2 tbsp maida (plain flour)
3 tbsp butter or oil
2 tbsp grated processed cheese
1½ cups milk
2 bhuttas (corn cobs)
1 green chilli - finely chopped
½ tsp black pepper
½ tsp salt

1. Pressure cook whole corns with 1 tsp salt for about 15 minutes on low flame after the first whistle. Scrape corn with a knife.
2. Heat butter or oil in a heavy bottomed pan on low flame. Add maida. Cook, stirring continuously, for 1 minute. Remove from fire.
3. Add milk, stirring continuously. Return to fire. Cook till thick.
4. Add boiled corn, salt & pepper. Remove from fire.
5. Add green chillies & cheese. Keep this thick paste aside.
6. Boil potatoes carefully on low flame so that the skin does not tear off.
7. Divide the potatoes into two, lengthways. Scoop out the potatoes. Keep the scooped out potato mixture aside. Butter the sides of the potato piece.
8. Sprinkle some salt all over, even the backside, of the potato. Fill the corn mixture in the scooped out potatoes. Keep aside.
9. Mix ½ of the potato mix of the scooped out potatoes with salt & pepper and a few drops of milk & cover the filled potatoes with this.
10. Bake for ½ hr. in a medium hot oven till the sides turn brown. Grate cheese on top and keep in the oven for 2-3 minutes more. Serve hot.

♣

Russian Sandwiches

Servings 4

4 slices fresh bread
4 tbsp thick cream - approx.
½ cup thick curd (of full cream milk) - tied in a cloth for ½ hour
1 carrot - grated
½ cup shredded cabbage
½ small kheera (cucumber) - grated
½ tsp mustard pd.
¼ tsp each of powdered sugar & pepper
3/4 tsp salt

1. Squeeze curd to remove liquid. Beat well to make it smooth.
2. Add all other ingredients, except cream. Mix well.
3. Gradually mix in the cream, taking care not to thin down the mixture. Cool the mixture in the fridge for ½ hour.
4. Cut sides of bread. Apply paste on all slices. Join 2 slices. Cut into two triangular sandwiches. Serve.

Mexican Burrito

Picture on page 54
Servings 5-6

DOUGH
3/4 cups maida (plain flour)
3/4 cups makai ka atta (maize flour)
¼ tsp salt
1 tsp oil

RAJMAH FILLING
1 cup red rajmah (kidney beans) - soaked overnight or 5-6 hours
1 big onion - finely chopped
2 flakes garlic - optional! - finely chopped
½ tsp salt
1 dry red chilli
1 tbsp butter
1 tbsp oil

HOT SAUCE

½ kg red tomatoes - blanched & chopped
2 onions - finely chopped
1 tbsp chopped spring onion
1 flake garlic - finely chopped
½ tsp salt
½ tsp ajwain (thymol seeds)
3 dry red chillies
1 tbsp oil

SOUR CREAM

1½ cups thick curd - tied for ½ hour in a cloth
2 tbsp cream
¼ tsp salt
3-4 tsp tobasco sauce

1. Sieve maida & makai ka atta. Add salt and oil. Knead to a soft dough.
2. Prepare hot sauce, by soaking dry red chillies in ¼ cup water for 15 minutes. Mash the chillies.
3. Dip tomatoes in hot water for 10 minutes. Remove skin. Chop.

4. Heat oil. Fry garlic & onions till they turn transparent.
5. Add tomatoes and mashed red chillies along with water. Cook till tomatoes turn pulpy. Mash well. Add ajwain, salt & spring onions. Cook for 7-10 minutes. Keep the hot sauce aside.
6. To prepare the filling, boil soaked rajmah along with red chillies.
7. Heat oil. Cook onions & garlic till pink.
8. Add rajmah, 2 tbsp of the prepared hot sauce, butter & salt. Cook for 5 minutes. Remove from fire & mash coarsely. Keep aside.
9. Hang curd for ½ hour. Beat well till smooth. Add salt, tobasco sauce and cream. Mix. Keep aside.
10. Make 6-8 small balls of the prepared dough. Roll out thin chappatis.
11. Cook the chappatis on a tawa on low heat, keeping the cooked chappatis soft in a casserole.
12. At the time of serving, heat the rajmah filling, spread little filling on the chappati. Pour a little hot sauce & then sour cream over the rajmah
13. Roll up. Fry in very little oil in a non-stick pan or a tawa. Serve hot with extra hot sauce.

Cheese Corn Balls

Servings 10

4 tbsp maida (plain flour)
4 tbsp butter
2 cups milk
½ tsp each of salt, pepper & red chilli pd.
4-5 tbsp fine bread crumbs - sifted
2 fresh corns - boiled

or

½ tin sweet corn - cream style
2 green chillies - finely chopped
2 tbsp chopped coriander
2 cubes (50 gms) cheese - grated
1 tsp chilli-garlic sauce

1. Boil whole fresh corn in salted water till tender. Scrape to remove the corn. Keep aside.
2. Melt butter in a heavy bottomed pan. Add maida.
3. Cook on low flame, stirring continuoussly, for 1 minute. Remove from fire.

4. Add milk, stirring continuously.
5. Return to fire & cook till a thick paste is formed. Continue cooking on low flame, stirring continuously, for ½ minute more.
6. Remove from fire. Add corn, grated cheese, green chillies, coriander, salt, red chilli powder and pepper. Cool the mixture for 10-15 minutes.
7. Add enough bread crumbs so that the ready mixture can be shaped into balls.
8. Roll balls in fine bread crumbs. Deep fry the balls on medium fire to a golden brown colour.

Note : If tinned corn is used, omit the first step.
Sift bread crumbs to get fine bread crumbs, which give neat balls on frying.

Paneer Balls

with Stir Fried Vegetables

Picture on page 72

Servings 4

PANEER BALLS

150 gms paneer (cottage cheese)
2 slices bread - sides removed
2 tsp curd
1 tbsp maida (plain flour)
2 green chillies - chopped finely
2 tbsp chopped coriander
a good pinch of mitha soda (soda bi-carb.)
½ tsp salt
¼ tsp each of red chilli powder, pepper & garam masala (mixed spices)

STIR FRIED VEGETABLES

½" piece ginger - chopped finely
1 carrot - shredded into long strips on the grater
1 capsicum - shredded into long strips
½ cup shredded cabbage

2 tbsp tomato sauce
2 tsp vinegar
salt, pepper to taste
1 tsp cornflour dissolved in ¼ cup water
2 tbsp oil

1. To prepare paneer balls, spread curd on bread slices.
2. Mash paneer. Mash bread slices and mix with mashed paneer. Add all other ingredients of the paneer balls. Mash & mix well.
3. Make 15-16 small balls. Keep aside till serving time.
4. To prepare stir fried vegetables, heat 2 tbsp oil. Add ginger. Cook for a few seconds. Add vegetables. Cook for 2 minutes. Add salt, pepper, vinegar & tomato sauce. Add cornflour paste, stirring continuously, on low flame. Remove from fire after a few seconds.
5. At serving time, keep vegetables on fire. Sprinkle some water on the vegetables. Add paneer balls, heat the balls for a few seconds, sprinkling more water if required. Serve hot.

Bread Patties

Servings 8

8-10 french beans - finely chopped
1 big potato - finely chopped
½ cup peas - finely chopped
2 carrots - finely chopped
2 green chillies - finely chopped
½" ginger piece - finely chopped
juice of ½ lemon
2 tbsp chopped coriander
1 tsp salt
½ tsp red chilli powder
¼ tsp jeera (cumin seeds)
½ tsp garam masala (mixed spices)
8 slices bread
3 tbsp oil

1. Chop all vegetables finely.
2. Heat oil. Add jeera. When it turns golden brown, add vegetables & cook covered for 5-7 minutes till done. Occasionally, sprinkle water, to prevent the vegetables from burning.
3. Add finely chopped green chillies, ginger, coriander, salt, red chilli powder and garam masala.
4. Cook for ½ minute on low flame.
5. Remove from fire. Add lemon juice & mix well. Cool the mixture.
6. Cut sides of bread. Dip in water & remove from water immediately.
7. Press bread carefully, keeping it flat on the palm, to squeeze out water.
8. Keep 1 tbsp of prepared vegetables on one side of the wet bread. Cover with the other half of bread.
9. Press well to give it the shape of a patty & seal on all sides by pressing.
10. At serving time, deep fry in hot oil to a light brown colour.
11. As soon as the patty is put in oil, do not touch it with the frying spoon. Fry 2-3 pieces at a time. Drain on paper.
12. Serve hot with chilli-garlic sauce.

Stuffed Spinach Loaf

Servings 4-6

DOUGH
1¼ cups maida (plain flour)
2 tbsp margarine or butter
4-5 tbsp ice cold water
¼ tsp salt
¼ tsp pepper
4 tbsp (1 cube) grated processed cheese

FILLING
2 tbsp oil
1 onion - chopped finely
1 cup chopped palak (spinach)
1 big potato - boiled and mashed
½ cup shelled peas - boiled
3/4 cup (100 gms) grated paneer
2 tbsp chopped coriander
2 green chillies - chopped finely
¼ cup fresh anaar ke dane (pomegranate seeds) - optional

½ tsp each of salt, pepper, red chilli pd. & amchoor (dried mango pd.)

1. Sift maida. Add salt, pepper, cheese & butter or margarine. Mix with a fork. Knead with ice cold water. Keep in a polythene in the fridge.
2. To prepare the filling, heat oil in a karahi. Add onions. Cook till light brown. Add washed palak. Cook for 5-7 minutes till water dries up.
3. Add potatoes, peas, paneer, green chillies & coriander.
4. Cook for 2 minutes. Add salt, red chilli powder, pepper and amchoor. Mix well. Remove from fire. Mix anaar ke dane. Keep filling aside.
5. Roll out the maida dough into a thin, rectangular chappati which is about 10" long & 5-6" broad. Spread some butter over the chappati.
6. Keep the filling in the centre. Fold the sides to shape it into a loaf. Seal the sides by applying a little water.
7. Brush the loaf with butter & bake at 200°C in a greased tray in a preheated oven for 20-25 minutes.
8. Prick a needle or knife in the loaf. If it comes out clean, the loaf is ready. Brush the ready loaf with some butter to give it a shine.
9. Cut into slices & serve hot with tomato sauce.

Grilled Mushroom Toasts

<u>Servings 8</u>

4 slices bread - toasted
50 gms mushrooms
1 tiny onion - chopped finely
2 tsp butter

WHITE SAUCE
2 tbsp butter
2 tbsp maida (plain flour)
3/4 cup milk
salt, pepper to taste

TOPPING
25 gms cheese - grated
1 tomato
coriander leaves

1. Cut mushrooms into small pieces.
2. Cook onion and mushrooms in 2 tsp of butter for 4-5 minutes on low flame. Keep aside.
3. To prepare white sauce, heat butter in a clean heavy bottomed pan.
4. Add maida and cook for 1 minute on low flame. Remove from fire.
5. Add milk, stirring continuously. Cook on fire until thick.
6. Remove from fire. Add salt and pepper to taste.
7. Mix the sauted mushrooms and onions in white sauce.
8. Cut each toast into 4 triangles.
9. Apply this mixture on each piece.
10. Grate cheese over them.
11. Garnish with a tomato slice and coriander leaves.
12. Grill for 5 minutes in a hot oven until light brown. Serve immediately.

Vegetable Cutlets

Servings 4

2 big potatoes - boiled
2 small carrots
10-12 french beans or ½ cup peas
2 green chillies - chopped
½ tsp salt
½ tsp garam masala (mixed spices)
½ tsp black pepper
½ tsp jeera (cumin seeds)
4 tbsp bread crumbs
4 tsp maida (plain flour)
oil for shallow frying
4 tbsp crushed cornflakes or bread crumbs to dust

1. Boil potatoes and mash them.
2. String french beans, scrape carrots.
3. Chop french beans and carrots finely.
4. Pressure cook beans and carrots with 1/3 cup water.

5. After the first whistle, pressure cook for 2-3 minutes more, on low heat.
6. Remove from fire. When cool, mash the vegetables. (If there is water, mash the vegetables on fire so that the water dries up while the vegetables are being mashed).
7. Mix mashed potatoes, green chillies, bread crumbs, jeera, garam masala & black pepper with the mashed vegetables.
8. From into heart shaped cutlets.
9. Make a paste of 4 tsp maida with 4 tbsp water.
10. Coat the cutlets with maida paste, roll in crushed cornflakes or bread crumbs.
11. Shallow fry in a pan or on a tawa till crisp and brown.

Spinach & Mushroom Pie

Servings 8

SHORT CRUST PASTRY (DOUGH)
200 gms maida (plain flour)
100 gms butter - chilled
½ tsp salt
4-5 tbsp ice cold water

FILLING
250 gms (2 cups) chopped palak (spinach)
100 gms (10-12) mushrooms - chopped
2 onions - chopped finely
1 tomato - chopped finely
2 green chilliess - chopped finely
2 tbsp oil
salt, pepper to taste
½ tsp red chilli powder
1 tbsp cream or malai

1. Sift flour & salt.
2. Add chilled butter. With a fork, break butter gently and mix with the maida. Mix gently with a fork and do not use your hands, because the heat of the hand will make the pie hard on baking. Then rub quickly & lightly with the finger tips till the flour resembles bread crumbs. See that the butter does not melt.
3. Sprinkle water evenly over the flour.
4. Knead to a dough quickly in a cool place. Do not over knead as the heat of the hands will make the pastry tough on cooking.
5. Chill the dough in a polythene bag for 15 minutes.
6. Roll out the dough in one direction only to ¼" thick, without stretching. The size should be 3" bigger than the baking dish.
7. Grease a 7-8" borosil glass dish & line it with the rolled out pastry, such that it covers the sides. Cut the sides in level with the dish. Pinch the sides to give a fluted edging.
8. Prick the sides & the bottom with a fork.
9. Bake blind (empty) in a hot oven for 15-20 minutes to a light brown colour.

10. Remove the pie shell from the dish after 10 minutes. If it is difficult to remove the pie shell, leave it in the dish. Keep aside.
11. To prepare the filling, heat oil. Add onions & cook till transparent. Add tomatoes & green chilli. Cook for 3-4 minutes.
12. Add washed spinach & mushrooms. Cover and cook for 5-7 minutes till done.
13. Add red chilli powder, salt, pepper and cream. Cook till dry. Remove from fire. Cool.
14. At serving time, fill the filling in the baked pie shell. Reheat in the oven.
15. To serve, cut into slices.

Note : If mushrooms are not available, use spring onions or leeks.

Cocktail Snacks
starters with drinks & soups before meals

Vegetable Shami Kabab

Servings 8

½ cup kale channe (black gram)
1 tbsp channe ki dal (bengal gram split)
3-4 laung (cloves)
3-4 saboot kali mirch (pepper corns)
½" piece ginger - chopped
1 dry red chilli
2 slices bread - dipped in water & squeezed
salt to taste
½ tsp amchoor (dried mango pd.)

FILLING
1 tbsp chopped coriander
1 tsp khus khus (poppy seeds)
1 onion - very finely chopped
½" piece ginger - grated finely
1 green chilli - chopped very finely
salt to taste

1. Soak kale channe with channe ki dal overnight or for 6-8 hours in 2 cups of water.
2. Pressure cook kale channe, channe ki dal, laung, saboot kali mirch, ginger and red chilli together. After the first whistle, keep on slow fire for 20 minutes.
3. If there is extra water, dry the channe for sometime on fire. There should just be a little water, enough to grind the channas to a fine paste.
4. Grind to a fine paste. Add soaked bread, salt, red chilli powder and amchoor to taste.
5. Mix all ingredients of the filling together.
6. Make a small ball of the paste. Flatten it, put 1 tsp of filling and make a ball again. Flatten it slightly.
7. Deep fry 4-5 pieces in medium hot oil.

Beans Mornay

Servings 16

1 small tin of baked beans
25 gms processed cheese
a few mint (poodina) leaves - chopped finely
4 toasted slices of bread

1. Cut toasts into 4 pieces.
2. Put beans on each piece.
3. Grate cheese finely over it. Top with a few mint leaves.
4. Grill or bake for 5-7 minutes. Serve hot.

Cheese & Potato Rolls

<u>Servings 16 pieces</u>

4 boiled potatoes - grated finely
½ tsp salt
½ tsp pepper
50 gms processed cheese - grated
2 tbsp milk

BATTER
¼ cup maida & ½ tsp salt, dissolved in ¼ cup milk

1. Grate boiled potatoes from the fine side of the grater. Add milk, salt & pepper. Beat well with a spoon till smooth.
2. Add cheese. Mix.
3. Make 1" long thick rolls. Flatten the sides.
4. Dip in a batter of maida and milk.
5. Deep fry 3-4 pieces at a time, on medium fire till golden brown.

Gingerly Paneer

Servings 16 pieces

200 gms paneer (cottage cheese)
1" ginger piece
1 dry red chilli
3/4 tsp salt
¼ tsp ajwain
juice of ½ lemon , ½ tsp oil

1. Cut paneer into 3/4" cubes.
2. Grind ginger, dry red chilli, salt & ajwain together to a paste. Add lemon juice and oil to the paste.
3. Rub this paste over the paneer pieces & keep aside for 5-7 minutes.
4. At the time of serving, grill on a wire rack, keeping an empty tray below the paneer, to avoid the oven getting messy by the drippings from the paneer. Grill till the paneer gets a little crisp and is heated through.
5. Sprinkle lemon juice. Pass a small fork like toothpick which can hold the paneer firmly, through each piece . Serve immediately.

Rice & Cheese Puffs

Servings 12

8 tbsp cooked rice
8 tbsp (50 gm) grated processed cheese
1 boiled potato - grated
2 tbsp chopped coriander
2 green chillies - finely chopped
¼ tsp salt
red chilli powder to taste
bread crumbs - sifted

1. Mash fresh or left over rice nicely to break the grains.
2. Add all other ingredients and mix well.
3. Make round balls and roll them in fine bread crumbs.
4. Deep fry and serve hot with minty yoghurt dip as given on page 133.

Kale Channe ke Kababs

Servings 12

BOIL TOGETHER

½ cup kale channe (black gram)
1 tbsp channe ki dal (split gram)
¼ tsp jeera (cumin seeds)
1" stick dalchini (cinnamon)
seeds of 1 moti illaichi (brown cardamom)
3-4 laung (cloves)
3-4 saboot kali mirch (pepper corns)
2 flakes garlic - optional
½" piece ginger
1 dry red whole chillies
1 onion - chopped

2 slices bread - dipped in water & squeezed
¼ tsp amchoor (dry mango pd.)
salt to taste

1. Soak channas and channe ki dal together in about 2½ cups water, for 6-8 hours or overnight.
2. Pressure cook channas with jeera, dalchini, moti illaichi, laung, kali mirch, garlic, ginger & red chilli to give one whistle. Keep on low heat for 20 minutes.
3. If there is any water left, dry the channas on fire, leaving just alittle water enough to grind.
4. Grind to a fine paste. Add bread, salt & amchoor to taste.
5. Chill the mixture in the fridge for sometime.
6. Make small flattened rounds.
7. Deep fry 4-5 pieces in medium hot oil. Drain on absorbent paper.
8. Sprinkle onion rings over the kababs. Garnish with chopped poodina leaves. Serve with yoghurt minty dip as given on page 133.

Note : If the kababs break on frying, add 1-2 tbsp of maida to the mixture. The kababs may also be rolled in maida & then fried.

Chilli Paneer

Servings 8

125 gms paneer (cottage cheese)
1½ tsp soya sauce
1 tbsp chilli sauce
2 tbsp tomato sauce
4-5 green chillies - slit lengthways
4-5 flakes garlic - crushed (optional)
1 tbsp chopped coriander
¼ tsp sugar
¼ tsp each of salt, pepper

BATTER
1½ tbsp cornflour
1½ tbsp maida (plain flour)
½ tsp salt

1. Prepare the batter by mixing cornflour, maida and salt. Add enough water to make a batter of thick pouring consistency such that it coats the paneer.
2. Cut paneer into ½" cubes.
3. Dip each piece in batter and deep fry to a golden brown colour.
4. Heat 2 tbsp oil. Fry the green chillies and garlic for a few seconds. Reduce heat. Add salt, pepper & sugar.
5. Add soya sauce, chilli sauce and tomato sauce. Add 2 tbsp water.
6. Add fried paneer and coriander. Mix well.
7. Serve hot with a tooth pick inserted in each piece.

Vegetable Roll-Ups

Servings 8

PANCAKES WITH EGG
½ cup flour
1 cup water
¼ tsp salt
1 egg
oil for shallow frying

PANCAKES WITHOUT EGG
½ cup flour
1 cup milk
¼ tsp salt
a pinch of mitha soda (soda-bicarb)
oil for shallow frying

FILLING
1 onion - chopped finely
1 carrot - grated
1 cup shredded cabbage

½ tsp pepper
¼ tsp sugar
1 tsp soya sauce - optional
salt to taste
1 tbsp oil

COATING
3-4 tbsp bread crumbs - sifted
¼ cup maida dissolved in ½ cup water

1. Mix all ingredients of the pancake to prepare a thin, smooth batter.
2. Heat a non-stick pan. Spread 1 tsp oil in the centre. Remove from fire and pour half of the batter. Spread immediately by tilting the pan with the handle.
3. Prepare 2 pancakes using very little oil. Cook the pancakes on one side only. Keep pancakes aside.
4. To prepare the filling, heat oil. Add onions. Fry till they turn transparent. Add carrot and cabbage. Cook for 1 minute.
5. Add salt, pepper, sugar and soya sauce. Mix and keep aside.

6. Cut each pancake into 4 equal pieces.
7. Place some filling on the side opposite to the pointed end of the piece of pancake. Roll partly to cover the filling. Fold the sides to seal the filling. Continue to roll upwards to form a roll. Seal the edges with the coating batter of maida and water.
8. Dip the roll in coating batter. Roll over fine bread crumbs and shallow fry 3-4 rolls at a time, in 2-3 tbsp oil in a non-stick pan till brown and crisp.
9. Drain on brown paper or tissue. Serve hot with chilli - garlic sauce.

Fruit & Vegetable Platter

Servings 4-5

1 kheera (cucumber)
1 carrot
1 radish (mooli)
1 apple
1 naashpati (pear)
50 gms paneer (cottage cheese)
1 tsp roasted jeera (cumin seeds) powder
1 tsp chaat masala
juice of ½ lemon
yoghurt minty dip - page 133

1. Cut vegetables, fruits & paneer into long slices. Do not peel the apple and the pear.
2. Sprinkle chaat masala, jeera powder & lemon juice. Toss gently.
3. Arrange in separate heaps in a serving platter.
4. Serve with yoghurt minty dip kept in the centre, as given on page 133, along with hard or soft drinks.

Vegetable Gold Coin

Servings 12

6 bread slices
2 small potatoes - boiled
1 small onion - chopped finely
1 carrot - chopped finely
1 capsicum - chopped finely
¼ cup chopped cabbage
1 tbsp chopped coriander
1 tsp soya sauce
½ tsp pepper
¼ tsp chilli powder
salt to taste
¼ cup maida dissolved in ¼ cup water
bread crumbs
oil for frying

1. Grate boiled potatoes.
2. Heat 1½ tbsp oil. Add onions. Cook till transparent.
3. Add vegetables. Cook for 3-4 minutes on low flame.
4. Add potatoes, soya sauce, salt, pepper & chilli powder. Cook for 2-3 minutes. Keep aside.
5. With a cutter or a sharp lid of a bottle, cut out small rounds (about 1½" diameter) of the bread.
6. Spread some potato mixture on the round piece of bread. Press.
7. Spread maida paste over the potato mixture.
8. Sprinkle bread crumbs. Press.
9. Deep fry in hot oil. Serve hot, dotted with chilli-garlic sauce.

Cocktail Sticks

Picture on page 53
Servings 8

1 boiled potato
1 firm tomato
1 capsicum
½ apple or 1 naashpati (pear)
¼ cup tinned or fresh cherries - optional
¼ tsp salt - to taste
1 tsp lemon juice
½ tsp pepper
a few toothpicks

COCKTAIL MASALA
2-3 sticks dalchini (cinnamon)
4-5 laung (cloves)
½ tsp ajwain (thymol seeds)
4-5 chhoti illaichi (green cardamom)

1. Grind all ingredients of the cocktail masala together to a rough powder. Keep aside.
2. Cut capsicum into long thick strips. Remove the seeds. Then cut the strips diagonally, into 1" triangular pieces,
3. Cut tomatoes & potatoes into 1" square pieces. Remove pulp of tomatoes. Cut apples or pear, with the skin, into ½" squares.
4. Heat 1 tbsp of oil on a tawa & put the potato pieces on it. Fry, turning sides, till brown & crisp on all sides.
5. Switch off the fire and add the capsicums pieces also with the potatoes & cook for ½ to 1 minute. Sprinkle 2 tsp cocktail masala, salt & pepper. Add the tomatoes and fruit pieces. Mix well to coat the masala on all pieces. Cook on fire for ½ to 1 minute. Remove from fire.
6. Thread on a toothpick, a piece of potato, then a capsicum, fruit piece, a tomato piece & end with a cherry if available.
7. Sprinkle lemon juice. Serve with drinks.

Note: The cocktail masala can be prepared in advance & stored in an airtight bottle.

Paneer Rolls

Servings 8

150 gms paneer (cottage cheese) - grated
2 tbsp maida
½ tsp red chilli powder
½ tsp roasted jeera (cumin seeds) powder
4 tbsp very finely chopped coriander
10-15 cashewnuts - chopped finely
1 tbsp kishmish (raisins) - soaked in water for 15-20 minutes
salt to taste (1/3 tsp approx.)

BATTER
¼ cup water
¼ cup maida
2-3 pinches salt
2-3 pinches pepper

½ cup bread crumbs - powdered finely & sifted

1. Mix paneer, maida, red chilli pd, jeera powder, coriander, cashewnuts, kishmish lightly. Add salt to taste.
2. Make 1½" long rolls. Flatten the sides to give it a neat appearance.
3. Prepare batter by mixing maida, water, salt and pepper.
4. Dip rolls in batter. Roll over fine bread crumbs & deep fry to a dark brown (not burnt) colour to get a crisp covering.

Cheesy Fingers

Servings 16

8 tbsp cornflour
4 tbsp (1 cube) grated processed cheese
1 level tsp mustard powder
½ tsp chilli powder
4 pinches mitha soda (soda-bicarb)
½ cup milk (approx)
1 tsp chilli-garlic sauce
4 slices of bread
oil for deep frying
salt to taste (1/3 tsp approx.)

1. Mix the cornflour, cheese, mustard powder, chilli powder, soda bi-carb., chilli-garlic sauce and milk. Mix well and add salt.
2. Keep this mixture for about 5-7 minutes. It should be like a thick paste.
3. Apply this paste over the bread slices on both sides.
4. Deep fry in oil. The toast should puff very well. Cut into finger shaped pieces. Serve.

♣

Chilli Potatoes

Servings 6

4 small (250 gms) potatoes
1 tbsp oil
2-3 green chillies
2 flakes garlic
2 tbsp salt
¼ tsp red chilli powder

MARINADE
2 tsp chilli sauce
1½ tbsp soya sauce
1½ tbsp vinegar
2½-3 tbsp tomato sauce
¼ tsp ajinomoto
½ tsp salt
¼ tsp pepper

1. Choose small sized potatoes. Peel them. Slice into ¼" thick slices.
2. Deep fry the slices to a golden brown colour on medium flame, so that they get cooked from inside while frying.
3. Mix all the ingredients of the marinade together.
4. Dip the fried potato slices in the marinade for 10 minutes.
5. Heat oil. Add garlic and green chillies. Cook for ½ minute.
6. Add the potatoes along with the sauces.
7. Add chopped coriander.
8. Cook stirring continuously, for 4-5 minutes. Serve hot with toothpicks inserted in each slice.

Refreshing Chaats
for all times

Aloo Chaat

Servings 4

4-5 boiled potatoes of medium size
1½ cups shelled, boiled peas
1" piece of ginger - chopped finely
2-3 green chillies - chopped finely
1 tbsp chaat masala (store the excess)
½ lemon
5-6 tbsp oil
salt to taste

CHAAT MASALA
¼ cup roasted saboot dhania (coriander seeds)
¼ cup amchoor (dried mango pd.)
¼ cup red chilli powder
¼ cup roasted jeera (cumin seeds)
¼ cup salt
¼ tbsp (kala namak) rock salt
½ tbsp saboot kali mirch

1. Prepare the chaat masala by grinding dhania, jeera, kali mirch and kala namak together.
2. Mix amchoor, red chilli powder and salt. Store in an air tight container.
3. Cut boiled potatoes into one inch square pieces.
4. Shallow fry the potato pieces on a tawa or frying pan till brown on all sides.
5. Remove the fried potatoes from the pan. Keep aside.
6. In 1 tbsp of oil fry ginger for ½ minute in the frying pan.
7. Add peas & fry for 1 minute. Remove from fire.
8. Mix potatoes, green chillies, lemon juice and salt. Add chaat masala to taste.
9. Garnish with fresh coriander leaves.

Corn Chaat

<u>Servings 4</u>

4 bhuttas (corn-cobs)
1 tsp roasted jeera (cumin seeds)
½ tsp garam masala (mixed spices)
½ tsp kala namak (rock salt)
1 tbsp sugar
1 tsp salt
½" piece ginger
2-3 green chillies
2 tbsp coriander leaves
1 tbsp (25 gms) imli (tamarind)
10-12 curry leaves - optional
¼ tsp rai (mustard seeds)
2 tbsp oil

1. Pressure cook whole corn cobs in water with 1 tsp salt till done. Remove corn from cobs.
2. Boil imli in half cup water. Strain and extract juice.

3. Grind ginger & green chillies to a paste.
4. Heat oil. Add rai and curry leaves.
5. Add corn, imli juice, ginger paste, rock salt, sugar, jeera & garam masala. Cook for 5-7 minutes.
6. Garnish with chopped coriander.

Peanut Chaat

Servings 4

1 cup peanuts with red skin
2 tbsp chopped mint (poodina) leaves
2-3 slices of tinned pineapple - chopped
chaat masala to taste
lemon juice & salt to taste

1. Roast peanuts without any oil in a karahi on slow fire, stirring continuously.
2. Mix mint, chaat masala, & salt.
3. At the time of serving, mix in the pineapple pieces.
4. Sprinkle lemon juice. Serve.

Vegetable & Fruit Chaat

Picture on page 71
Servings 6

2 boiled potatoes - cut into 1" cubes
1 small kheera (cucumber) - cut into 1" cubes
1 tomato - cut into 1" cubes & pulp removed
seeds of one fresh anaar (pomegranate)
1 banana - cut into slices
1 apple - cut into cubes without peeling
1 tbsp chaat masala or to taste
juice of 1 lemon

1. Deep fry potatoes to a golden brown colour.
2. Mix all ingredients.
3. Add chaat masala & lemon juice. Toss gently. Serve.

Potato Baskets

Servings 6

3 medium potatoes
3 tbsp cornflour
1 tsp salt
2 small wire-strainers
oil for deep frying

FILLING

1 cup sprouted moth
1 onion - finely chopped
1 green chilli - finely chopped
2 tbsp chopped coriander
¼ cup khatti chutney - page 134
poodina chutney - page 135
½ cup curd - beaten well
chaat masala - to taste

1. Peel, wash potatoes. Grate them. Add 1 tsp salt.
2. Keep aside for 10 minutes. Squeeze to remove water.

3. Add cornflour. Mix well. Heat oil in a karahi. Take 2 metal strainers.
4. Dip in oil. Spread some potato mixture on one oiled strainer. Press with the other strainer.
5. Keeping the strainers pressed together & holding the handles carefully from the end, dip the strainers with the potato mixture in hot oil. Fry till golden.
6. Remove from oil. Loosen the sides with a knife. Gently tap the strainer to remove the basket. Cool the baskets to make them crisp. Prepare more baskets similarly.
7. To prepare the filling, steam sprouts in a pressure cooker with 1/3 cup water and a little salt. As soon as the first whistle starts, remove from fire. The sprouts should be on fire for 4-5 minutes only.
8. Cool sprouts. Add onion, green chilli, coriander, salt, red chilli powder and chaat masala to taste.
9. Fill baskets with filling. Pour some beaten curd to which a little chaat masala has been added.
10. Pour some poodina chutney & khatti chutney on it. Serve.

Dips & Chutneys
to serve with snacks

Yoghurt Minty Dip

Serves 6

1½ cup thick curd
1 tsp oil
1 flake garlic crushed - optional
1 tbsp paste of mint leaves
½ tsp powdered sugar
¼ tsp mustard powder - optional
salt, pepper to taste

1. Hang curd in a thin muslin cloth for ½ hour.
2. Beat well till smooth.
3. Add all other ingredients.

Note : A little cold milk may be added in the yoghurt dip if it appears to be too thick.

Instant Imli si Khatti Chutney

Serves 6

1 tbsp amchoor (dried mango pd.)
3 tbsp sugar or shakkar (gur)
½ tsp roasted jeera (cumin seeds) powder
¼ tsp red chilli pd.
¼ tsp salt
¼ tsp garam masala
3-4 tbsp water

1. Mix all ingredients together in a small heavy bottomed pan.
2. Cook on low flame, till all the ingredients dissolve properly and the chutney reaches the right consistency.
3. Cool. Serve with Indian snacks.

Poodina Chutney

Serves 6

½ cup poodina leaves (½ bunch)
1 cup hara dhania (coriander) chopped along with stem
2 green chillies
1 onion - chopped
1½ tsp amchoor (dried mango pd.)
1½ tsp sugar
½ tsp salt

1. Wash coriander and mint leaves.
2. Grind all ingredients together with just enough water to get the right consistency.

Coconut Chutney

Serves 6

½ cup freshly grated or desiccated (dry pd.) coconut
¼ cup roasted channa or channe ki dal (split gram) - roasted
1 green chilli - chopped
1 onion - chopped
3/4 tsp salt
¼" piece ginger
1 cup sour curd - approx.

BAGHAR
1 tbsp oil
1 tsp sarson (mustard seeds)
1-2 dry red chillies - broken into bits

1. Grind all ingredients of the chutney adding enough curd to get the right consistency. Keep aside in a bowl.
2. Heat 1 tbsp oil. Add sarson. When it splutters, add broken red chillies.
3. Pour the baghar into the chutney. Serve with South Indian snacks.